December

Julie Murray

Abdo
MONTHS
Kids

abdopublishing.com

Published by Abdo Kids, a division of ABDO, PO Box 398166, Minneapolis, Minnesota 55439.
Copyright © 2018 by Abdo Consulting Group, Inc. International copyrights reserved in all countries.
No part of this book may be reproduced in any form without written permission from the publisher.

Printed in the United States of America, North Mankato, Minnesota.

052017

092017

 THIS BOOK CONTAINS
RECYCLED MATERIALS

Photo Credits: Alamy, iStock, Library of Congress, Shutterstock

Production Contributors: Teddy Borth, Jennie Forsberg, Grace Hansen

Design Contributors: Christina Doffing, Candice Keimig, Dorothy Toth

Publisher's Cataloging in Publication Data

Names: Murray, Julie, 1969-, author.

Title: December / by Julie Murray.

Description: Minneapolis, Minnesota : Abdo Kids, 2018 | Series: Months |
    Includes bibliographical references and index.

Identifiers: LCCN 2016962346 | ISBN 9781532100260 (lib. bdg.) |
    ISBN 9781532100956 (ebook) | ISBN 9781532101502 (Read-to-me ebook)

Subjects: LCSH: December (Month)--Juvenile literature. | Calendar--Juvenile literature.

Classification: DDC 398/.33--dc23

LC record available at http://lccn.loc.gov/2016962346

Table of Contents

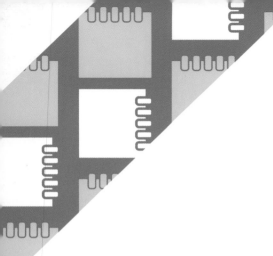

December

There are 12 months
in the year.

January

February

March

April

May

June

July

August

September

October

November

December

5

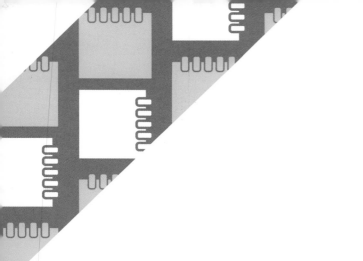

December is the 12th month.

It has 31 days.

December

1	2	3	4	5	6	7
8	9	10	11	12	13	14
15	16	17	18	19	20	21
22	23	24	25	26	27	28
29	30	31				

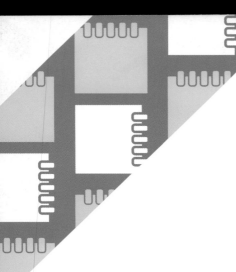

Walt Disney was born this month! He was born on the 5th.

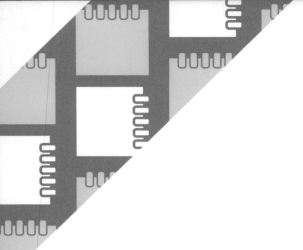

Winter begins in December.

There is less daylight.

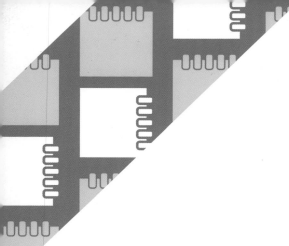

Mia lives in New York. It can snow a lot! She helps shovel.

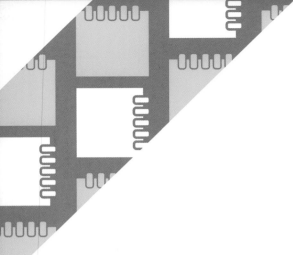

Eli celebrates Hanukkah.

She lights a candle.

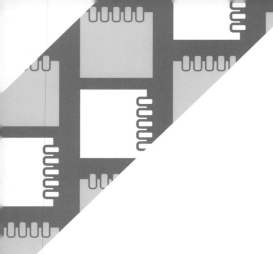

It is **Christmas** on the 25th.

Tim got his mom a present.

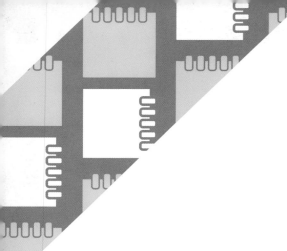

Kwanzaa begins on the 26th.

It lasts for seven days.

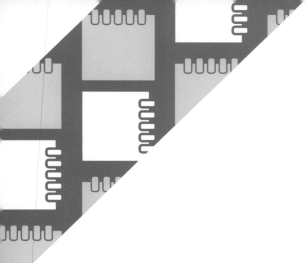

Sue gives the snowman a nose.

She loves December!

Fun Days in December

National Cookie Day
December 4

National Day of the Horse
December 13

International Tea Day
December 15

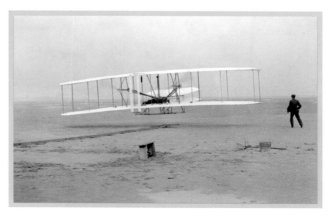

Wright Brothers Day
December 17

Glossary

Christmas
a Christian holiday celebrating the birth of Jesus Christ.

Hanukkah
a Jewish holiday lasting 8 days to celebrate the rededication of the Holy Temple.

Kwanzaa
a holiday to celebrate the cultural heritage and traditional values of African Americans.

Walt Disney
an animator, voice actor, film producer, and businessman, who created Mickey Mouse.

Index

abdokids.com

Use this code to log on to abdokids.com and access crafts, games, videos, and more!

Abdo Kids Code:
MDK0260